THE ONE-STRAND RIVER

RICHARD KENNEY

THE
ONE-STRAND
RIVER

ALFRED A. KNOPF   NEW YORK   2008

THIS IS A BORZOI BOOK
PUBLISHED BY ALFRED A. KNOPF

www.aaknopf.com

Knopf, Borzoi Books, and the colophon are registered trademarks
of Random House, Inc.

A list of previously published poems appears in the Acknowledgments.

Library of Congress Cataloging-in-Publication Data
Kenney, Richard.
The one-strand river : poems, 1994–2007 / by Richard Kenney. — 1st ed.
p.   cm.
ISBN 978-0-307-26763-4
I. Title.
PS3561.E443O54 2008   811'.54—dc22   2007044321

Manufactured in the United States of America
First Edition

In memory of my sisters,
Carolyn Clare Kenney and Alison Kenney Hall,
this book is for heroes and muses remaining:
Hollis and Will, Carol and Maeve, my family.

Gray goose and gander
Waft your wings together
And carry the good king's daughter
Over the one-strand river

CONTENTS

PART ONE

THE
WATER CLOCK

PEN, LINE

Here a heron's bill
poised above the still tide pool
where no gulls lament.

Horizon rings red,
and around the seabird's webs
monofilament.

HOW I USED TO WISH

How I used to wish—
watching out across the wet roadbed's
black glide—oh, the usual,
shell-shore of the first world
willed back in a blink:
lingcod, then, thickening the ocean like
life with time. . . .
                No time, by God!
Good night now licking
eyelids up in some immense sleep-swimming
immemorial armored fish,
fusion mirrored there on that flat nerve,
novas and so forth, symmetries,
this smattering of energies,
G-force veering to the simple
solipsism of the born stars: Sol
mating with himself himself in that fresh
electric swamp where further fetch-candles
kindle away all wavery and settling,
long before nylon stockings ever
were or lunatic desire
seared us, just void,
volts and amps and the blue hiss—
isn't it?—and then that's this.

ORRERY

Or, Concrete Delivery Delayed
by Goose and Gosling Crossing,
Late March, Mallett's Bay

Right here the season's first clear pavement's geyser-
ing a slow New England spring: zinc culverts
Hooosh, awash; ditches, moats; toads' argots
Smirching the gusty winds and sloughs where birds mince
Wordless through reflected skies, and here, in vertical
File, strut, slap, this goose and nine piddling goslings
March the yellow centerline, where clemency
Comes down with the clutch in the sky-high cab, diesel
Manifold gargling tuning forks in the ugly lingoes
Of big trucks, hot stack puffing up another silty
Heaven over slow revolutions, loose cement
Sliding, sliding, sliding its wet drum sling,
And nothing in the whole world hard or straight
But the driver's eye and the goose's gait.

REAR VIEW

At 90 on I-90 out of Anaconda,
Montana, a lone deinonychid biker—look,
He's passing: he's taking the road like a dog on a leg,
Or the flatulent jump of a Thompson gun. . . .

Condor neck, gray mane a coronal storm
Around his plastic yarmulke—the logos
That pate sports relate mostly to the holocaust
Between his legs, the verbs for which he's said "to be born."

His own shanks canted high as a birthing mother's
Leave him in semireclining elegance.
Claws clung up wide high like Christ's. Fringed leggings,
Jerkin, gauntlets, thongs—he's clothèd all in leather.

I watch his flogging shadow, thrown noon-low
Below the chassis. It writhes like a count's cape
Caught in a belt sander: so the paved
Miles howl by, and who'll alone

As on a Harley or a desert island not gape
A little in the rear-view mirror? Meanwhile, the fringe
On his saddlebags whips nicely. Inside . . . a syringe?
A Glock or two? Ibuprofen? Books On Tape?

A flick of the wrist, a puff of blue, and this god's
Gone. Thoughts of the road. Long thoughts.

SKY WITH EAGLES

Now the sky is aching blue and clogged with eagles,
The nappy sea smoothed and carded by a kite-breeze
Too good for a kid, who'd waste it wondering

Nothing: God, how some days we feel all oracles
Must augur wrong, all history a blink of surprise
Before us, alive, alive, and no wintering

In the heart, and no dimming, no closing
Ever of the eyes, of any beloved's eyes
Anyway, never that black-ice-like sundering.

GRASSHOPPER

Now we rope-a-dope a just-post-mid-August lost cause.
Now we flounce into the hammock, collar up, craws
Stuck with the hollow bone of winter whistling. Denial
Is us. We cringe in lemonade. We horrible gaily smile.

LENS

Even as green summer bends
Through the garden window glass,
Rippling to its end in thin
Isotheres somewhere over
The Gulf, where contrail snows,
Where dragonfly feels wind shear
Following the hummingbird—

Or as the whole wrinkling star-
Field's foil on some collapsed sun's
Unseen, matte, prismatic curve,
Where even time's tent dimples,
Where atoms frail as Chinese
Lanterns catch in a mind's cold
Coriolis, adder's coils

Closing, as the garden scene
Draws close around it green glass
Of the rainy window now,
So summer's wrung memory
Corrects through this flint lens, love's
Also, chromatic, slight, sweet
Heat-shimmer, hummingbird's wings.

CURRENCY

Blazing glory of the summit sun!—
But it's already twilight in the ferny valley, since
Time is Altitude.

Endless day: jet like a bangle
Sun-hung, while the world spins under, since
Time is Longitude.

Icicle on the lilac, look—
And a letter from Tampa, where spring is old, since
Time is Latitude.

Now?
Loose change in the pocket.
Watchband loosens on the wrist.

ALBA LAPSE

Dew is smoking off the roof,
All spider lines alight,
Each clover eave is dropletted
With a little crystal lute.

The lichen, likewise, and the moss
As mown grass underfoot
I've tracked across linoleum
Unlacing a soaked boot.

The coffee is insinuous
As also in the nose
Is wet wool, and wet dog,
And even more nuanced

The veil of dewfall boiling off
The fresh-cut cedar shakes—
But that was quite some time ago.
Oh, for heaven's sakes.

MORE LONGITUDE

Mariners, too, dead reckoning, ply

The deep blind. The bearing's known—westerly,
Always—but never the miles remaining. Celestial
Techniques prove unreliable. The breast-
Plate covers the chronometer; no solace
There. Still, we loosen the collar and listen. Still,

We make a private study of the sky.

THE ONE-STRAND RIVER

Here is ring terrain,
And here is ring marine.
This is the lower troposphere
In the Middle Holocene.

This is a water clock.
This is a green rain.
This is a sundial filed sharp
On the slant of the sunlight's grain.

Look, a watchwork iris;
Here, its bronze spring.
I think of the story of Osiris
Figured on a ring.

This is an eye unblueing,
The copper green, change;
Here is the tide of the one-strand river
Lapping ring terrain.

Gray goose and gander
How long have we together?
Green, the memory of love
As blue, a change of weather:

Rain, rain, rain
Scattering down the sky
Where heart's an armillary sphere
Of rainbows in the eye.

Now the water clock
A trickle under rime,
And oh I fear for the good king's daughter
Crossing over time.

I stand on the bank of the one-strand river,
River blue nor green,
And where is now, with the good king's daughter
Over ring marine?

FOR MY SISTERS

PART TWO

RIVEN HEAVEN

.

OCCULTING

Orb, we know, a fob, attaches to a stopwatch,

Brute biology of aging, which
While bearable, brings worse: whingings,
Wan imaginings, shyings from the jinx

Dumb chance, with more or less pheromone,
May come to seem, in time. It's not the fear
Of calendars, exactly. What remands

Rue? The niggling worm?—that durable worm,
Licking like a blessing the sunlight off the morning,
The skin of sunlight, thin and always forming

The shapeliness of things? Ought we go out cowled,
Cassocked, monkish, muttering, gum-suckled, so-and-so-called cuckold
Of the bodily clock? Or uncork champagne? Occult's

No cult, but just the natural darkening of the world.

NEW

You've heard?—incredible! A second moon!
How was it discovered, then? No one?

No. . . . No. . . . I've not seen it, either. "Zither-
Silver," whatever that means. The azimuth

Is indeterminate, whatever that means.
Why can't they speak English? What use is a moon

You can't court by? What are "receptor sites"?
They mentioned the blood's love for carbon monoxide,

By way of example. They say the problem isn't
Optical, exactly. The moon's unrisen

Quality is artifactual
Of structures in the ancient brain: one jewel

Occupies the setting, so to speak;
The nerves won't crimp around another. What keeps

It there? Why can't we blink the old white cinder,
Then, surrender

To the new? To see a moon not "new," but *new*?
I'm asking me, I'm not asking you.

NOTES TOWARD THE NEXT QUESTION

Clear enough a culture's questions, more than its answers,
Define it?—that's understood. How many sublunaries dance

On the perch of a pin? It isn't as though we've *measured*
That. It's just that the substantial nature of angels isn't major.

Hereabouts. Nor no more whether the Pig God Phug
Will successfully inseminate the moon. Forget

About the bawdyhouse of the corn. It doesn't signify.
And if I

Suggest more pressing issues occupy our clergy,
Such as the missing mass of the universe, dark energy

And so forth, well, question our assumptions,
If you will. All linchpins shear. Some chance

Ours may. Then what? Tentatively: hap hulip scong monk.
Hoop, π, diddlepom plunck?

TURBULENCE

On his deathbed, Werner Heisenberg declared that he will have two questions for God: "why relativity, and why turbulence." Heisenberg said, "I really think He may have an answer to the first question."

There is of course the nervous question of the airfoil;
Laminar flow over headphones where wave-torque
Puddles the brains of my seatmate—awful

Rockaddle—also, missing shards of crockery tucked
Behind our unplugged refrigerator, as bits
Of Mars, it's said, are littering Antarctica.

Consider, too, the impudence of fluids,
How when my double gurgles off the little iceberg
Of its highball, one drop often finds the eye. Follow it

Where the penny, bouncing from the urban cobble, spark
In a pocket, arcs elsewhere, and winds up spinning
From the Bridge of Sighs. Let's say God's spigot

Needs a washer, which you, while explaining
Physics to a friend, supply. *Chaos,*
is all, you yawn, sleepily—not in the splenetic

Literary-critical sense, requiring Icarus
To fall and fall and fall, but rather in the rinsing,
Sundog, water-scatter sense, here in the cirrus

Of it all, that pure ebullience we're (as
The bubbly flight attendant says) experiencing.

THINGS

The scent of soap
As she went by
Lent me hope;
I can't say why.

And the little laugh
In the young man's eye
Was fully half
Of the blue of the sky.

Are these things *things*,
Or nothing at all?
What's a thing?
What it recalls?

RESONANCE

How might the Arcturans
view
my memory of you?
No trance,
but trace:
not that still-warm, breeze-
riffled roadkill
I'd call *Life*, imprecisely,
love-sot in the old toad-
kissed anthroparochial
coign of vantage,
but rather that sledge-
touched, light-curdled sacerdotal
bell of the brass world whanged
again on one of its jillion
resonating, wincing
frequencies—
a chord,
a frisson,
songlike, kin to the chill
priest-whistle
rhyming with itself in the high, stone-winged
belfry of the pelvis,
cell recalling sea-pool, viscous
with time . . . if memory like physics were all
what, no *who*,
then *O My Love*, I'd whisper and say,
and this would be detected from space
as a resonance wave of the world,
echoing you.

SONG

If eros were an orrery
We'd wind its little crank
And set it spinning, bud to bloom
To fall, to stark blank.

If eros clocked its seasons so,
Each life would pass them through
And start nowhere and end nowhere
As many clearly do.

Would you say love's a water clock,
Or one wound on a spring?
Or spun by hung dependencies
As is most everything?

The weakest of attractions runs
The universe; they found
It takes a ball as big as Earth
To pull a person down.

Then Einstein showed that gravity's
A shape and not a force,
Which may explain the awful fall
We took up off all fours.

Though where that leaves the orrery's
A question left to verse:
If eros has its seasons, then
For better or for worse

As waves to shores or tears to snow
Or luck to muttered charms
Attraction as a shape returns
Us to each other's arms.

SHALL I COMPARE THEE TO APPEARANCES?

I check my watch. 8:10. You paint an eye, blinking
In the dubious glass held up to the Christmas party,
Turning back the clock. You are very pretty,
But also beautiful; but what I'm thinking

Is: *Rainier.* Invisible all month behind a veiling
Weather one wouldn't have thought could cloak a moth-
Wing, well, tonight the ancient volcano, big as the mother
Of all mother ships, shows its alien

Glacier to the moon. It looks close enough to lick.
And how much worse than a lamppost, that. And all along,
Who cared a fig for anything but the long
And short and heavy and high and wide? Here's to the relic

Of the what else, wet on the nerve, and what compares?
Numbers?

0,1

Well, but that was before riven heaven,
That was before you thundered on the earth,

Little boy, wet and sudden as the birthday
God turned a pocket inside out, spilled night

And the moon's shiny dime . . . it's a new moon's
Dated, indistinct features minted on it sun-

Wise, ready to be thumb-rubbed over time
Into such sharper focus as this short world's whorled space

And time permit. . . . Oh, that was before you thundered
On the earth, third man among us, lightening

The earth's pull on your mother and the moon's on me, who together
Teased the threads of fundamental things apart,

Parting waters like lovers like the black nothing
Of the stars' interstices, and everything,

The whole of it, bigger, believe me, the close cosmos
Opened that day, and a great pleat opened in my heart.

2 A.M.

You are a moon-washed mer-personage
of the first waters.
Now you are a showily crucially outspraddled eagle
of the startle.
Moreover,
you are a surefire niche
market. You are nothing if not a little otter.
You are a murmurous moon-miss of a wriggle.
You are one burped girl,
and no other.

EPICYCLES

Damn the epicycles,
what time is it? I've been
awake for hours. Seagulls
on the roof like bison.
Beside me here, my son
mutters in Sumerian,
something charming, some-
thing about the beginning
of things, putting me in mind
of the idiot chuckle of teletype,
sudden printer chatter, fax-hiss, fuss-
budget sleeplessness of machines
in the hairy ears of sleeping watch-
men in the middle hours, in lit-up
offices and darker offices,
far from this awful place.

                    *

Damn the epicycles,
what time is it? I've been
awake for hours. Machine-
hum, moron
Freon mantra. Mice scutch
pink fiberglass above. Below, burglars rummage,
spill kitchen matches,
gargle brandy, piss in
the sink. Mars's
thumbed mite smears the window. Seagulls
stumble on the roof like bison.
Beside me here, my new son
mutters in Sumerian,

something charming, some-
thing about the beginning
of things, the black nuisance
of God's insomnia,
what came of that, affixed
for all time, black, in ink,
putting me much in
mind of the night hilarity of teletype,
sudden idiot printer chatter, of fax-
hiss, fierce sleeplessness of machines
in the hairy ears of sleeping watch-
men in the middle hours, in lit-up
offices and darker offices
far from this awful, dead-
bolted, sheeted vigil, this awful wish-
torn, dumb, bed-
ridden god's gurney—
poor, haggard, wing-shot god
whose knee-joints ache with the space between bones,
the body separating, hammer and anvil full of the unsaid,
the never, the whine of gone
souls, hum, like that, like the refrigeration
of the dead.

                 *

Damn the epicycles,
what time is it? I've been
awake for hours. Seagulls
on the roof like bison.
Beside me here, my children
mutter in Sumerian,
something charming, some-
thing about the beginning
of things.

PART THREE

URANIUM ROSE

ALBA MINE

Now night's abandoned diamond mine's
Been dynamited open, love.
Crickets creak like weakened timbers.
Waken now in a vein of love.

Love, the slick on the eastern sea's
Meniscus now is red again,
Is upward sun's unbreaking egg
Bled together and round again.

Again the mountain-crumpled moon's
Losing pressure in the black tree,
And now it's just invisible,
And now is breeze in the black tree—

A button at your open throat—
A button at your loosened sleeve—
A kiss crushed and all red
And roar of the sun in a slipped sleeve.

NO ODDER ELSEWHERE

Elsewhere, the ten-thousand-year-old methane hurricane on Jupiter;
A putative diamond hailstorm (this is imagined to be literal) on Neptune;
Live geysers on Europa; nitrogen snow on Triton.
Olympus Mons, beside which Everest would seem a wart, on Mars.
Here, just this. Upthrust of human love on Earth.

SQUALL CORRELATIVE

That quick cloud-pleated
sky that swung exploding

chandelier
that delirium

that green-crazy
flimmering tree that frog chorus

kerosene kilt
occulted sun sudden skillet–

hiss upon
upturned cheek and hard rain-pocked pond

that wind-wrung hive of leaves
midsummer eve's

lightning ozone
that uranium rose

and that's not all.

NO.

Look about you, folks, I say. No roads
Here, amongst such succulents and hung lianas
In the sun's flooded wheel-rut . . . right:
Take notes. What do you *feel?* The fen yawns. . . .

Distally, at least, it's not all hearts and flowers,
Jots John, from Planned Parenthood. *Baroque . . .*
Irrational . . . not infrequently weird . . .
Worse: here the poled pirogue

Of Humanism slips the everglade
Of endocrine function, doing
Its very best. The frictionless glide,
The tour group *ahhing* and *oooing,*

Background bogwhine, insect
Slap and a little smeared blood. Question:
Can mind solve sex
As a cursive symbology of force, wished on

The Darwinian star by
Tactical prayers of a selfish gene?
(Croc to starboard.)
But someone always interrupts: Sheena

In a leopard pinafore, poutily
No, no, say rawther the WON-
derful irrationality of sex!—prettily
Smiling, as a water moccasin winds

Around the pirogue pole, which I drop. If
Only . . . But now we are perfectly adrift.

NOT COLLEGE, RECALLED

Itch unexhumed: *in the dim patchouli-*
Fields of the deep stacks—skirt-stirred strata
Lit only in the fungal flicker of tube-light, the jewel-

Glim ruby of the emergency auxiliary power unit, pitch-
Blende at the navel of the medulla-dancer, dull rotor-
Valve of the thuddering chest, Persian luxury—*parched*

Galumph finds love! Lo the Dewey-eyed librarian
Shakes down her hair! Spun onyx! Raven cataract
Fine as ever river reverses itself to surf, a prayer

On parted lips! Alabaster scapulae! O rare
Lapsarian lucky rapt protean boy stalled in the salt sea-wrack
Of his worst intention! O ylang-ylang! Aureolae!

Hell of the endocrine, unkind, leg-long, finger to lip and almond
Eye! O hell of the too too long soon simoom sin mind!

CONSTITUTIONAL

Dog walk, with coffee, wrist scalding awash, leash
Smoking like harpoon line toward the tortoiseshell Persian
Licking her left front paw with such absurd composure
Behind the left front tire of the Chrysler. Churlish
Thoughts bedevil me, often. Sunshine; girls
Half my age; the future; unseen perishing
Armies; cloud-scud like scraps of lingerie;
Taxes. I keep to the middle way, with neither Chihuahua
Nor wolfhound. The cat bolts for the broker's Porsche.
Birds continue to practice their hideous lechery
At every branch and cloud, which I acknowledge—*joie*
de vivre, I call it, constrained as I am, rich
In little but the imaginary, bourgeois
To the bone—which we'll return to presently, pup, in the fridge.

SURREALISM

Skillet bottom rule-straight prairie releasing a little
To a ripple of sand hills, side-lit

At twilight, called The Palouse. Note again schooling fishes
Nosing the windshield, uffish

Through the sunroof. Whites pooled at the bottoms of my eyes,
I watch a spiky caudal fin surmise,

Ripple, and disappear. *I hate surrealism,*
You say, sullen. *How do you feel about nonsense, lissome*

One, I rejoin, adding *Ghogli woolly scrooly lo.*
Och, wholly different, family and phylum! you yell, Oh

You prefer History . . . deep History,
The *really* used to, the *true,* the *facts,* austere,

Where the sand hills of the Palouse surippidly rumple on
Like the pink roof of the doggish yawn,

Formed as they were in the tidal Ice Age estuary
Of an ancient glacial outwash, where

We speak, right here, and above,
To a depth of a hundred feet at least, my scurrily love.

COMPOSITE

Who, then, that one who says
his Hometown USA's
a digital composite?
Count: the old porch rocker;
Grandpa with his posset;
sudden and recursive
sift of winters; sitcom-
flicker, blue in the draped rhomboid
yawn of the neighbor's bedroom;
dog-bark down the block. . . . Black-
top cooling in the rain and the rain-blink
memory, all this ruminant
cud culled from the immensity
of the single disintegral city,
Childhood, God bless this one, amen.

COMMUNICATIONS SYSTEM

Again asleep. Again awake.
A city far away: key-quick
My love sends me telegraphy
Along the sheet

No languid arm, no taut leg
No slippery with moon, alack

No AWACS plane relays a wave
No pheromone unfurls its whiff
With more efficiency than this
Distant beat

No fishes parching in their thirst
No sonar since the Tethys Sea

No walkie-talkie copter chop
No damn subdermal circuit chip
No digitation dit-dah-dit
Could so cede

The sense of being lip to lip
Or send a laptop signal up

Any sweeter, any quicker:
Love, this life is just a flicker.
I'm alone.
Hurry home.

THE ROUGH

They're in the very rough of love;
Clubs couldn't part 'em.
                    —*As You Like It*, misremembered

Such love stuns
Does sit like mad on the Maypole of the spine
Spindrift ice storm to the clicking eyelid
Lit or sudden sun

Comes each ragged in the customary
Store-bought ostentation
Urgings of this kind require:
Quarrystone skies, drumskin stammering

Prairie wind, wheat laid white,
Eye-white also, teeth on teeth,
The mare's hooves striking divots,
Everywhere heaven overplaying, light

All Jacob's-laddery, rock horizon
Zoom baring its single snaggle denture,
Jar of fireflies, nakedness in rain,
Arrant ludicrous strutting unreason

Of divinity . . . I'm
Not saying my love is necessarily a goddess but that Goddess
Does undeniably down
Don her flesh from time to time.

TO CIRCE

Oh to live ignobly!
Not pig-
Like, quite, nor bleating,

Braying, mewling, really;
Neither, though, thoroughly
Morally:

Not for a life of pure sensation
Per se,
But certainly a little freer of those cleansing agents

Applied to the topsoul
As to a porch stoop
With such Dutch zeal

As leaves all dream raw-red
And smarting. Duty! Horrid,
Overwrought rat-

Tail file, drawn like a fiddle-
Bow across the faithless
Heartstrings. . . . How fatal

It'll feel, at the moment of choice,
Or how could we—Jesus!—
How could we breathe? Such joys

Rest
As your paw on mine, my sweet cat, my erst-
While sorceress:

History's an open sewer.
Worse:
I miss you, wer-

Whoofed again into the animal,
Liminal
Life of a landstruck sailor man.

PART FOUR

FOLLIES

ALBA BOATS

Again, the elements
Of a typical morning in the marina:
Bell buoy; brants and guillemots;
Bill's elder sister in a

State in the outside shower, bawling
The choruses, humming the verses,
As usual, "Deutschland über Alles,"
For the reliable if various

Effect on the transient moorage patrons.
Up at the pancakes and coffee,
Maraca-rattle (Motrin),
*New York Times*es (goofy

As ever), one Ludlum, two Clancies, and an Edna
St. Vincent Millay.
Mud in your retina!
Seize the day.

MILLENARY

I wish for no cars, coalfires, clang-
Clang nuclear alarms, or only electric motors
For the Great Mother, and we had ten-speed recycling
And aquaculture bars, and the great circle
Closed again, and golden eagles eagling.
Wouldn't it be great if jobs were sweaty and outdoors
And people lived so simply nothing was lacking?
Wouldn't it be perfect if every man could hammer
His own nail and every woman hem
Her own hem? And vice versa? And backpacking.
Wouldn't it be better if we could just live in harmony
With our own energy, and with nature's millennial rhythm?
Oh, wouldn't it be grand if there weren't too many
People in the world, and I was one of them?

AESTHETICS UPDATE

The seams of the Technological Sublime
Have been pretty well mined out, don't you agree, on the little
And the big screens? And the awe of volatiles
In oxidation, surely. Boom, boom. Blame

Hollywood. They did it. They wrecked us, right? Wrong. Sang-
Froid did. We're unsusceptible to Beauty in its terrible
Guise. We are big reptile guys. Unutterable
Doesn't cut it anymore, if you know what I'm saying.

Occasional volcanoes in the parlor, yawn. Arterial
Blood weeping the walls, rising above the ankles
Curdles in the drains and pupils. Ad nauseam! It kills
Sensation in the extremities. And don't come off all teary

On me, now. No more *Thus Spake Zarathustra*. No big titanium yurt
Over heaven. No more swoopy blue yondering wing-magics—
That's finished. We don't feel for thingamajigs
Anymore. Clear your desk. And tell the engineer he's fired.

AIR SUBLIME

Up in First Class, the gorgeous flight attendant
Is breast-feeding a middle-aged man in a cashmere
Sweater, tassel loafers, and amber-tinted,
Squarish glasses. Back here, the whole schmear

All over again about not giving oxygen
To the baby first, the float cushion, the awful
Video with their heads between their legs. Such an
Insulting—look, the chap with the matchstick Eiffel

Tower over there is being told he'll have to place
It in the overhead compartment. He's starting to cry,
He's that mad. "I'm sorry, sir," is said, with a straight face.
But as I was saying, it's so insulting. This is the *sky*

We're going to, for heaven's sake, unless the pilot misspoke
Himself. It's not *about* headphones and Coke.

VOLKERWANDERUNG

or, *From, Originally*

(Coffee black and pie, please.) Look: gawkers,
Doughy varicose *tourists*, recent
Arrivals, by the look of those new J. Crew cargo-
Pocket shorts and Rockport walkers, houri
Wives in sunscreen lipstick, raisin-
Eyed, mugging, ex-Montessori
Slumping sons in backwards baseball caps, *Whoa,*
They pantomime, missing the truly chilling vegetable
Fury in their sisters' eyes, whose
Flesh swells under little braided spancel
Anklets—lo, the trans-American family, lo-cal colas,
Killer grins and all. Not that back table
Though, a tight clot of *real* folk, Buffalo-nickel
Locals, all inside hats and Rapunzel
Hair and whinnying mean ironies
Who, not having been in the technical
Sense born here, aren't original anywhere.

NOW WE ARE READY TO SPEAK OF BODIES CHANGING INTO OTHER BODIES

At Abergroupie & Fetish
The young people just
Can't keep their pajamas
Up. Neither modish nor faddish

The boys look like licked pecs;
Chicks also, with that slapped-
Around, feral, solipsist
Chic. In Ovid's epic-

In-scope work, the tongue
Stuck to the mirror, didn't
It? Whatever. The forbidden
Fruit's sox in the trunks,

I think. Gap gone bad. Ipecac
Gaze. They do look pretty tough,
Bagged, rampant and mounted. Stuffed
Animals. Gel over kapok,

Whispers Mr. Hemingway
Here, from behind the arras.
He says you bet your ass.
But they're cute as minxes, ink-way.

METAMORPHOSES

1. BAD NEWS, GIRL

He's so *complex*, she says, meaning something
Like he doesn't call so often, thinksome

As a brick, really, he drives a Boxster,
Preening bastard, and picks up girls at Starbucks

On their way to work. Double lattes
No-fat-triple-skinny-half-caff, like that, till it's

All smiles and then a hard drink or tumble.
It won't work out. He lives in Baltimore . . .

Bullroar, that's not why, that's totally backwards.
I think I love him, she says. Take those words back!

You don't want this one, girl, he's pure bad news
For you, *n'est-ce pas*? He's a noose, he's a nosebleed,

He's *married*, you little idiot! It's only a *Miata*!
I'm so lonely! For pity's sake, will you look at *me*?

2. NON SEQUELAE

Watch!—this man is in a bad way: when
A fine woman swims into his ken

His heart swamps with such suffusing grief
It's scuttled utterly upon the reef

53

Of love. Not just aflutter, but undone.
Undistinguished story, thus far, but for one

Refinement: when this happens, he will spin
And follow. Not stalking. Not a sin,

He thinks, his scans sufficiently askance,
Discreet, and from a gentlemanly distance.

No speech. His need, according to the Law
Of Never Me, of course: to find a flaw,

Permitting, first of all, his pulmonary
Function to return. And then, to bury

That breach of what perfection might have been
With all its non-sequelae squarely in

The necessary realm of Never! Never!
No way! Unh-uhhh!—nevertheless averring

Life still bearable on such terms. Meanwhile,
Watch: he's done it again. The lighter step. The smile.

3. NOT WANTING, WONDERING

How would it be, she wonders
To be ravished by so evidently violent an animal? The thews . . .
The neck as thick around as her waist . . .

How would it be, he wonders
Idly, nightly with not one but two
Sets of twins?

They sit side by side under
Low heaven, shifting a little in the pew.
She's imagining something that makes her wince.

Gas, he thinks. The price of gas. Imagining this and/or
That configuration, he dabs his philtrum. Flu,
She reflects. A touch of it. Or perhaps the liverwurst.

Have they done their worst? It isn't what you'd call a waste
Of shame, exactly, but none of it's anything anyone wants.

4. I LOVE NEW YORK

Sex is diverting in the opening rounds;
Later, it's power that holds the attention.
                                —Mme. Mao

Love, which is to say Romantic Passion—
What else was there, ever? Victory,
I guess, there's that. That's it, except Repose, and
There's a state from which a roach evicts

A prince: too fragile for the robust taste.
Which leaves Love, and Winning Big—both cool
In certain phases, surely—the first, tough, bust-ass
Vows; later, the Lexus and the heated girl

(*Pool! pool!*—a jejune quip, so sorry,
Reader!)—But as long as I have you on the line,
May I inquire into the ossuary
Of your own life's joy? Your anodyne?

Cat got your tongue? Oh, never mind. I'll swear
You were with me last night, warm as dinosaurs
Have turned, in the last ten years or so. No, Officer,
I'll say, she was right here, center aisle, wearing

Red, as usual. We'd dressed and dined
(Brace of quail and tiramisu, wary
As we were of the creme brulee) and lo—blind
Luck!—walked into the poetry reading. Pure sorcery,

If I do say so. Where were we? Well, gorillas
Grok what dissidents and advertising bastards,
Vulgar as they are, call Power; schoolgirls,
Too, and boys, since Paranthropus robustus

Left the veldt for good, driven to extinction
By short guys, as usual, the big goof. As for opening rounds,
And didn't I ask you to pour me a drink? Hun?
What were we talking about? I said *sit down.*

VOLKERWANDERUNG AGAIN

While the girl silently mouths *Shut up*
The boy is muttering computer apps.
Mom dumps a lot of NutraSweet

Into Pops's orange cup.
Granpops shouts about the Japs
Again, and gums his oats. *Eat,*

Mom sternly to the smirking kids cajoles.
Then peeks to see who's heard, like a turtle,
A little. Meanwhile,

This vacation founders on other shoals.
The dog is out of Synthroid. There is a turd
In the motel pool, the boy smiles

To report. The Subaru needs servicing,
As does Mom, who bears up. Pops's
Problem is certainly no *worse.*

YOU SEEM A LITTLE NERVOUS
Yells Granpops. The girl begins to sob.
Pops starts to speak, then demurs.

LIGHTNING STRIKES THE PROTEIN-RICH
POSTCAMBRIAN TIDE POOL

While not a Wiccan coven, quite, the local
Food Co-op's a colloquy
Of gray braids above those wool felt clogs

One wise woman over there—no nubbly
Linsey-woolsey leggings, no loose Andean
Knitwear on *that* one—stylish, undeniably

Above this war of worlds—calls don't-fuck-me shoes.
Here at the Sinclair station, other issues
Rule. Recumbent with dunces, as usual, we're a who's

Whom of never, ever gracious to a fault,
Phallocentric, smoky, sulky with Miss Oil Filter,
September '85, abulge with those brick-sized billfold-

And-belt-chain gentlemen's accessories
One always sees in philadelphias of this sorry
Sort. Anyway, across comes a girl in Minoan axes

Asking Do any of you comedians want a Quinoa
Or Spelt Flake Smart Drink? No one
Blinks. Got kamut? offers Phil. The *sine qua non:*

Contact. Civilization begins anew.

NEW YEAR, WITH NIPPERKIN

And so the world begins again
In mild disarray
Where the best-laid plans of mice and men,
It's said, "gang aft agley."

"Gang aft agley"—that sounds just right—
Strangulated, glottal,
Where violence meets backwardness
Summarily throttled.

So merrily and merrily
The Monday doth embark
Us on another work whose week
Will leave us in the dark,

A drink in hand and Parkinson's
Or worse, maybe, to stir
The ice into its carillon
Of Larkinsense and myrrh:

More light! More weight! More love! Less hate!
The Mass, the Seder, ah
The tools we use to disconfuse
Ourselves, etc.

And so, to bed. I draw the shade.
Should auld acquaintance croak
They're none of mine, nor "Auld Lang Syne,"
Whoever he is.*

* Joke

FINAL EXAM

No joke. Do you follow? No furlough
From this one. It isn't as though

The show will be over ever, and they'll
Be coming back for a curtain call all

Smiling and relaxed. We won't be ad-
mitted backstage tonight, or ad-

journing anywhere comfortable after.
Think how you've laughed it off, as if

Spring brings your hair back, or the
Beginning of a new school term turns ortho-

pedics upsy daisy. The scales tip
Toward the heel: your step's steeper

Today, no?—your eye milkier, your mind (poor
Wretch) a cooling porridge

In its pot. You haven't thought forever
Through, yet, friend, not really—far-off,

Formal thought, you've thought!—you haven't
Thought that through, nor worse, what heaven-

less, pitiful, cold, culled comfort
Memory is. Your mother's smile? Your own first

Cupped breast or sobbing fraternal commiseration
Or motorcycle skid or shapely curveball missed

Or hit into the stands, whiz kid, your dad's
Dry hand that day, and the handsome graduation gown?

Gone? Here's a short quiz: *Who's dead?*
Good. Now put your pencil down.

PART FIVE

ARS LONGA

BALANCING

Sweep linoleum. Set table. Rain and the bestial dark.

To be honest, as in the case of Noah's
Tough call regarding the mastodon (the Ark
Yawing offshore, that awful trumpeting) we've nowise

Equipoise. It never was a balancing act:
The smart primate with the broomstick on his nose
Looks right, and the plate set spinning—accurate

Too, as far as it goes. God's
Finger, just off-canvas from where you're at—
That's what's missing. The ghost

Of his whorled print's still visible in the wood
(All wood, of course, easily seen in cross
Section) honoring the Tree, whose forward

Pitch, like the push broom's pitch, like yours, can only increase
As a function of time. Physics has a word for
This: intopplery. Most falling's less Icarus-

Like than acornlike: the pitching up to oak-and-
Over, oopsy, slow. Romelike. So, despite appearance, then,
All standing's falling, really, reckoned

Over time, if stalled a little in the labyrinthine
Cochlea (or else that smoky hot maraca,
Human memory, though that's another lapsing

Altogether, never mind miracles).
Where now the broomstick man, sprinting laps
Around his badly wobbling plate, remarks

The worrisome eccentricity of its ellipse,
Decaying now, worse than Mercury's
Weird orbit, or . . . think of all the space-junk God lobs

Over the brink each morning before breakfast—Mach
Twelve is all it takes to miss the stone horizon,
After all. . . . If a tree falls in the forest . . . curious

Old philosophical saw, conflating reason,
Sensibly, with the double function of the inner
Ear. Equilibration . . . sensation. . . . Rise and

Fall. . . . Where was I? Oh yes: I'm dead, and it's time for dinner.

SOME CHARLES AND A FRESH START

When I was one and nothing, christ-
ened in the apse of what happens,
I was pretty Carl
Jung, all yin and blinking eyes—

There's an image.
Turn the page:

At twenty I kissed
My own ring, I was a prince
Of chuffing rolling stock, I was Charles
The Hammer, I had hat size,

Oh, I was wide-gauge.
At double that age

Change: I was a blind unicyclist,
Ray Charles
On the night pond's
Black ice.

What a stage.
God save me from rage

Anyway, if sixty comes, eyeglassed
All too clearly once again, pince-
Nez by Carl
Zeiss

Scared old: *courage*
Richard, old churl, whose rib cage
Echoes a little still, iconoclast

Tapping at the valve: be Boris Karl-
Off bolting upright on the soapstone lab bench, sawbones
Staggering back, aghast, again, by Christ!

PER BENJAMIN FRANKLIN

As per Cole Porter,
When torpor

Or implacable whim fly
In the face of reason, why

We follow them!
What then when

It turns out Reason, perforce,
Verse-

Perfect, has taken the shape of the world
As it truly is? Well,

Oof,
That's Life.

Tough
Luck. You should've

Thought
Of that.

Next time make a list, two columns,
Cons

And *Pros*.
And next life, do it in prose.

POETRY

Nobody at any rate reads it much. Your
lay
citizenry have other forms of fun.

Still, who would wish to live in a culture
of which future anthropologists would say
Oddly, they had none?

SAXON RIVETS

Doubtless I should have dressed more sincerely,
Sans rhyme, that gentleman's accessory.
Sorry. Had I only more appropriate garb . . .
Gabardine. Gods, why didn't I . . . I do not deny
Denim, or the quantum laws of Fashion or Chance.
Jeans have I also, and other costly folderols
Folded in my philosophical armoire.
Were I to steeple my fingers in apology,
Polish again would indict me. Why don't I Just Do It
Dude. Moot
Meter. Read
Rude: my new mode. Back to basics:
Saxon rivets. This verse—this is not pseudonymy,
No, ma'am. This is a suit.

EYE IN A FINE FRENZY ROLLING

Scions of CEOs and Trappist
Monks, poets practicing youth
In a pierced and studied *contraposto*,
Streetwise always to this couth
Thought: nothing true or possible

Big. Excepting of course its anorect
Reverse, the ironical, catheter-
Threaded cant-
Cant curse, goth-
Awesome—hear it?—the dry cigarette-

Cough of the Cumaean
Sibyl: *Looky!—It's nothing!*
It's never! It's gone!—
And under the eyelids the luna moth
Banging, and the big world's lion yawn.

ITHACA

As we—how to put this—*get along,*
Call it, and it becomes clear our foibles are less ex-
Charming foibles than forms of mental illness

Shedding their softer outer layers, Uncle
Fool and Aunt Cracked in all their feckless
Bone shine eroding to the surface—nozzles

Of the family DNA writhing our enervated
Grip—well, our loved ones will simply have to cope.
Myself, I do not anticipate this problem. Mind

You, I *am* something of a veteran.
These piercings—porcine shipmates—Circe's poke—
That settling wreath of moly smoke. . . . Still: dime-

Thin, I'm a jogger, sugar. I'm a power-sylph. I'm
Fine. I've never felt so much myself.

MORE CHARLES AND AN OLD STORY

TESTAMENT

I who have no god and no elders
To my spawn *per stirpes* the fourth part
Of this unfinished tale unto the smelter
Of gone smile and sullen art:

CORPUS

What Darwin wondered once upon a time
(Less Mendel's elemental mirror-rhyme) . . .

Whereunder furs Neander and Lascaux
Bore offspring Ovid's verse would video . . .

Whence Aristotle's golden middle starts
A story God'll finish in three parts . . .

Why, we're chimerawise in time: instinct-
ual each metonym, mind, heart or sting—

CODA

How are we to form a sentence
Space and time remember, Sibyl?
Selves of heads or tails or tense
In solvents so immiscible?

A dragon, over time, evolves
His own Saint George, by subtle forces
Understood since cold cavewalls
Redfigured metamorphosis:

Who slew all queer unnaturals
In the flume of change, in dark reflection?
The father of these children, Charles,
The deicide. So, by selection

Must we monstrous integrate
Our gryphons from what hairy wethers,
Eagles bald and plantigrade
And lions of a different feather

Fill those forms half recognized
If foggy in the shaving mirror:
Father's nose; a daughter's eyes;
Old Bones, unmythical chimera.

BIOGRAPHICAL

As with optics, so verse:
The barrel of the instrument
Provides the focal length (self-
Adjusting, alas), but not the focal point.
The life's light's necessary vessel,

Surely. Surely bits and pieces
Of biography refract
Into the work. Perseus
(Who used a reflecting scope) in fact's
No poster boy. Now you see us,

Now you don't. Consider: why
When I raise my arm to point, a stone's
Throw or a star's away, a widened
Thought—a fire—a face—a distance—
Does my dog gaze at my finger? Don't.

LIVES OF THE ROMANTICS

Byron holding a skull considers sutures
Awash in claret, which he tosses off—cheers—
Refilling his odd goblet yet again. Such

Searching passion! Such idiosyncrasy! Listen: his palazzo
Whistling with hypochondria, cats (lots),
Cockatoos, monkeys, and a bear. Opalescent

Peafowl swaddle the *piano nobile;* urchins
(Leigh Hunt's) hid Lord Byron's special chirurgical
Orthopaedic boot behind a chintz

Chaise. Shelley's elsewhere. Here's Shelley
In water and fire. (All these things actually
Happened. Have you ever clawed a vessel off a lee shore?

No? Then shut up about Shelley.) Imagine parakeet
Swoop over candle: that's green wave over bare spar.
Days later, they knew the body by the Keats

Close-folded, breast-pocketed. Keats, purest
Of them all, a seaway also, brine-writ,
Aspirating brine. Byron, wren-wrist

Of another lovely Venetian *principessa*
Caught in his pincer, purses
His lips. Trelawny reaches into the pyre of friendship,

Palms the meat heart itself—which ends up
Ashes in a sachet at her throat who opened
The vein of awful goth novels, all hells hence-

Forth racked worldwide in pharmacies.
And speaking of Coleridge, the mercy
Of his means, that old glass-and-cat-fur

Hair-up charged quality he brought to all occasions—
He got old. As Wordsworth, walking Oc
Angry, lithe like Blake's cat uncaged—

Curtains. Mt. Blanc caught him, too; he withered; he's gone.
Keats is drowning over the sunken Barca, delirious.
Escorted home on shipboard by Tita, Fido-true, his gondolier-

Bodyguard, Byron's body bobs, preserved
In wine. As all these poets are—priests,
Really, religious services being as usual whatever oeuvre

Requires of them, a fishy-deep, a furnace-
Heart. And we? Latter-day supplicants, too, Nosferatu
At the coffin, sucking the wine. Ah, to

Deserve the Romantics! *Live like Shelley,*
Write like Keats, said another poet, who surely
Meant *Die like Shelley*—but now I'll shut up about Shelley,

Having done none of it, myself.

HOW AM I?

Certain worldlinesses for which I've chafed,
At earlier times in my life, to reach
Well past, while secretly—O Icarus!
Poor Richard!—

I've, for a little of it, at least, at last achieved
Something like a genuine disinterest. Roshi,
Is this progress?
Take my temperature.

PART SIX

METAMORPHOSES

ALBA UTTERLY

Now homeworld whanged hard:
melted glass-spatter everywhere. Weird

big theropod
things all whuffling and thudding.

Birds littering the rain like wet ash.
Ocean

boiling in a few places. Pinned
corsage of the first flowering plant opening

its vulva to the rain—
something like that, for a change?

CONSOLATIONS OF VERSE

At my house, it's coming to be understood
That in the increasingly dubious neighborhood,

The as-yet-largely-unnegotiated polity
Which is my son, something is about to . . . appalling

Thought. Left not a little paler by the nowhere-
Near-vague-as-yet sumptuary

Memories of my own adolesc—but never
Mind all that, for Pete's sake. Even Miniver

Cheevy for all his pathetic folly tippled
To preserve the world as it hadn't been. Pallid

The leash-men: that's Dad, I expect. Who's in season?
All I know is, all I know is, my beautiful son's

"Stretching out," as they say, and silencing, and darkling,
And it's eleven, and the seventh-grade girls are circling.

TALENT SHOW

Former Cub Scout furrows brow like bull Klingon
Bathed in tungsten. All is klieg light. So nice,
How someone's son (eighth grade), preparing to sing,
Transforms!—is sudden priest of Dionysus!

Like . . . like . . . anorectic mantis-walk! or

Orang in rut-cum-neuromuscular-twitch,
Face a mask, some satyr-rage-rictus-orc
Like, say, scrotum locked in the teeth of an Eleusinian witch,
Or something, or much too much homework.

How can Progenitor account for such a cloud?

In what coin can unquiet heart requite?
Assuredly, emotion toggles. Rock's rock. No doubt.
Boggled Father feels bad, but knows not quite
What about.

ANOTHER UNFORTUNATE ENCOUNTER

We suspect that one over there disapproves
Of us. Little hints.

There are of course reasons to disapprove
Of us. But since

He couldn't know any of the good ones,
We suspect him of unrigorous

Thinking, and find ourselves suffused, once
Again, with vinegar and ichor.

REWRITE

The *Metamorphoses* are changing, ladies
And gentlemen. (Is this microphone working?) Leda's

Not the only bird who's going to get ungoosed,
Here, and never mind *de gustibus*

Non disputandum, damn the pedophiles,
Abuse is abuse, to the devil with all godawful

Reifying myths, and that includes those boy-crazy
Goddesses (to be fair) here at the Borghese.

Think!—think of the invidious figures Ovid's etched
In history: take the Gorgon, differently-visaged

Enough to stop a clock—she's a doozy.
Few need re-visioning as Medusa does. Seducers,

To turn the other cheek, deserve to be coerced.
(*Vide MLQ; GQ;* all vols.) Consider the worst:

Bernini's infamous sculpture, *Hell and a Girl:*
Forget technique, if you can, the action-figure swirl,

Sheer drapes, the marble dimpled like a pudding
Where hard hand vices thigh—off-putting,

All of it. Retitle it *Like a Rock: Hell, Bent:*
Dead White God Dissed—no, say *DisEmpowerment:*

Patriarchal Boundary Violation and the Erotics
of Darkness. Now fix it: Bernini's rewrite, all karate-

Kicks, spandex Lycra, lithe as Jackie Chan's
Rubber sister, she pastes him in the main chance

(*Yessss!!*)—and it's a whole new ball game. Ceres
Smiling, winters amiss, no more miseries.

Well it's true, in California, before the sack.
I'll take a few questions now. *Yes—in the back?*

MORE WAR SONGS

When Heliodorus Peplos wrote
Seek not songs from the Scythians, but swords,
Variously translated (crawl in the street

For cobbles, not rubies, etc., in the general sense), he was sued
(Pseudonymously) on behalf of the Boreal Barbarian Bard Guild
For Wrongful Inferential Defamatory Vox, absurd

As that may sound to the contemporary ear. "Gaoled
Was Heliodorus for his tongue was sharp" (Gibbon). No one's
Suggesting that he shouldn't have been killed;

Feelings were hurt, that much is certain, if only in Athens. Whence
Our knowledge of Scythian Bards, drunken, collegial
In their way, and whose songs now seem, truly, to be nuanced.

CHALLENGES & OPPORTUNITIES

The luncheon's done. Like gas dirigibles,
Endowed professors drift about the room.
Development officers nibble cheese. The rich
Crouch, waiting for the lights to dim.

Someone thanks someone, who takes the mic
And thanks us all again. He introduces,
Amply, one who'll introduce the Reich
Of a thousand years or less, downsized. Sousa's

To be replaced, we learn, by !Kung plainsong,
Which seems only prudent. Seamless cross-disciplinary
Interfaces will be initialized via live cam, along
With distance learning, in real time. The plenary

Session of the legislature—applause—if feasible.
A sub-dean begins to gibber like the Sibyl.

DAPHNE ABDUCTED

While the first book, *Young Men Without Irony*,
Had secured her career, the second and subsequent works
Lacked dash. Bicoastal marriage; child with a runny
Nose; the underperforming 401K—irk-
some, certainly—yet all these were as nothing,
Next to the nagging ache of homesickness
Suffusing space halfway to Rigel, the mothwing
Moon on her cheek, crescent sun a cirque
Of nucleons releasing from the tear duct
Of the lorn Arcturan vivisectionist
Bent close above, his forceps and retractor
All agleam. Her last thoughts were of sex—an anise
Scent of medicine—all unfamiliar, in
The way that everything had always been.

SCENES

1. THE HALF-MUSTACHE

But hadn't they been going to take another stab?
Nothing's easy, but you have to try. . . .
She, luggage at the threshold, too erect.
He, briefs and shaving brush and half-mustache, a wry
Attempt at. . . . *Don't come out, you're not dressed.* Indirect,
backlit against the headlights of the cab.

2. A FALL

It was so easy to pluck up the dropped package—*Are you hurt?*—
take his elbow, and help him to his feet. Pauseful
then, she saw the old fellow seemed to be ashamed. . . .
Old fellow, she burned to say, *it's no shame
to be an old fellow!* But then she saw in his impassive
face that he wished to eat her heart.

3. BIMETALLIC CORROSION

They parted at the dock. Words were muted.
She left with nothing, of course. That she'd tossed a purse
of pennies into the bilge . . . we'd naturally thought
the gesture a gloss on his famous parsimony,
not . . . he, with the sixty-foot aluminum yacht.
It settled months later, in a hundred fathoms, off Bermuda.

IMAGINATIVE LITERATURE 101

Here's Pluto crippling off like a bent plowshare,
Underground again for good. Here's Ceres,
Smiling like Gertrude Stein in a miniseries,
Explaining about no more winter. *Thanatos,*
Excuse me. Lose the pomegranate, toss
The rice, and don't go caviling it's not *true,*
What's that anyway but a construct. If CO_2
Emissions hold steady . . . well, summer everywhere!

(This poem, too, is running out of air,
And not for lack of pluck, but rather thumbs
Feeling for its windpipe. Apothegms
Like *You wouldn't think it was so freaking funny*
If what happened to that poor girl Persephone,
Like, your wife, or daughter. It's a freaking nightmare.)

THE CARBON CYCLE

I. BEGINNING

At Orvis, the discontinued *Coal Miner's Pant*
Is offered for sale again this season
As the *Upland Field Pant,*

Available in my size.
So came I to step into this pant
[Cat. # 000; Wheat; Long Rise]

Sockfoot, beltless, trepanned
In the three-way changing-room mirror. Wry-
neck, then, Procrustes' guest bent

Sidewise so to fit this glass gallery's
Low gaze. Bituminous pupils opened
Wide. *Abandon hope.* I felt the lyre

Curl in my elbow like a cat. I knew
That song. I swallowed hard, and I stepped through.

Three of me, that is, reversed,
And closer than I appeared. Like a privacy
Curtain, the mirror rippled a little behind. Before—Carboniferous

Silver!—a soughing of moon-fronds, fulgent vesper
Of the tree ferns. . . . Cuffing is free at Orvis.
Seeds catch there, sometimes, little burr-

Like pods. I potted one, if only to prove its
Provenance. Go ahead!—by all means, try the berries.
I did. And whether Hell or Elsewhere, there on the verso

Side of smoke and mirror, eerie
As it all seemed, the weirdest thing, the marvel of marvels—Orvis,
Beanstalk, dream-aerie or Mesozoic Era,

Whether dark be light or moonset in the east—
Was how those trousers draped, and held a crease.

2. END

Just joking. This is, after all, Orvis's
Story, not Narcissus's, who—that novice
Alice, no hellhound either—never

Made it past the mirror's mercury,
If that's the silvering still used in rivers. Kore:
She's the one who plumbed that black sulfuric murk

First, of course, sheer corn. Recall?—Persephone,
Sweet flowers in the coalshaft, seismic love, softening
Resolve, hell ahead like an open purse,

Poor lassie, straining for a sky dime-sized
And dwindling . . . what a tale. Or else Eurydice's—
Similar, if different—your dizzying

Tumble, reversed erotics, etc.—
Though a sadder one, certainly, since she's deceased

Year-round. Love's a puzzle,
Isn't it? Consider its apostles:
Paris, Perseus, Helen in a parasol . . .

Everybody loves myths, especially metamorphoses,
The ones about relationships. Forces
Of nature: mass times velocity, with a human face.

What's your name again? Hold up the mirror:
Here's a fun house for you, more or
Less as figured in the *Ars Amatoria,* rare

As tears: imagine, say, our famous tale, reversed,
Denatured, chopped, regendered. Rivers
Of Darkness. The steep, heart-chattering climb. The Rift

Valley. Black light. Stark hero,
In khakis and a blazer, ablaze. Act I: stock horror.

Act II: our hero, having offended some sky-
Headed god or other (never mind which, or why;
We don't know that story), sentenced to half his seasons in whiskey

Smoke and cold torpor (posit hell, here, a nether queen
And so forth. Fill it out)—he's sequined
Suddenly in sunlight—his second chance, forsaking

Others, to climb back into life! One catch (the Orphic
Part): his love must never ever waver in her gaze, or—
That's the thread he climbs, you see. A fig

For either of their chances. Act III: the dramaturge
Directs attention to the rim of trauma:
She, now, kneeling downcast at the jewelled edge,

Heaven's wellhead. He—well, that's suspense. A tease,
As ever, toward Eventualities.

What's next? What nicks the singing E-string
Of her far horizon? Princely equipage? A plumed crest? A strong
Possibility. Will she . . . ? Oh, no. Oh, hell. Oh well, Easter

Erases this myth anyway, and what's a myth
But a young fairy tale, and what's that but moth-
Dust of the gone wing, belief, and when that's gone, too, arrhythmias

Of breeze and bloods and seasons supervene.
Biology's reliable, that old parvenu,
Who always finds a peace for which to sue.

Thus Love, like lawyers on a climbing wall, willed
This. When a fairy tale tears, it's not like faith, or failed
Troth, but only a return, a little drop back into the world

As it always was, old sport, polled ox, once told,
Retold.

3. MIDDLE

Hemmed here forever a land of alterations, cuffs
Unfinished, collars turned. Who's the fairest?
The mirror, like a methane glacier on Callisto, calves.

Here forever the giant mycelium forest
Populous with big cobs
And dachshund-sized silverfish, fierce

Flowers, like *that* one, just now snapped shut on a goblin-
Lemur. Look, some kind of black digestive nectar
Leaks out, smoking. Wipe its chin. Blintz-

Soft tube worms upholster a sulfur vent. Naked
Rides the moon on the pupil's cistern.
Night tightens like a tourniquet.

[Copulate. Desist.
Note not yet to what or whom you turn.]

PART SEVEN

WESTERN WIND

MUSE INTERVIEWS

I

Nationality?—ah, I see, *Roman.* Too bad.
You looked promising. You'll have nothing to write about,

However, having been raised in what we're calling "bourgeois"
Circumstances—suburban, even, I see. And the Porsche

Finishes it. My advice? Ha!—be born
In Illyria, bad Alba, Transalpine Gondwana, the barrens

Of Pictland, in the black gauntlet of tyranny.
Boot on the neck, barbed wire at the sealed frontiers

Of pain, if possible, that's what a poet wants.
That's the Tower. For you?—the corrugated Quonset

Hut of contempt, I'm afraid. Ac-centuate the trivial.
Show Rome for what she Really Is. Reveal

Silliness and shallowness. Irony and small anger,
These must be your tools. And of course the ingrown

Suppurations of your personal life. That does it. Any questions?
Good luck to you, then! *Next—*

2

What?—"The West"?

That the governing notion of Roman don't laugh virtue
Is at stake and changing? That the world is at several big verges

Of Roman devising? That we still have a plausible apocalypse
Under the prairie and steppe? That this might properly eclipse

Certain other grave geopolitical issues which,
In the balance of possible pain, amount to whinging?

That the world is a world of ideas, and the consequential
Ones these days are mostly Roman? Not just quenched

Revolution, the jewel of liberty darkening, the quaint
Constitution shelving, nor, elsewhere on campus, quantum

Cosmogony's queer whirligigs and their friable backwash,
Or the goggle-eyed sorcerer's apprenticeship swashbuckling

The gene pool, nor Narcissus in silicon grinding a mirror
Of the human intelligence, nor elsewhere the grumble of armor

In the desert, the howl of the jetfire in the kids' heads?—
What's your point? Where's the suffering? You heard what I said.

WHITE PAPER

The jobless rate continued to decline.
Presidential Bulls (e.g., *No Child Left Behind*)

Backfired nicely. The Guild of Girls Next Door
Had by this time driven the professional whores

Into a subset of narrow specialty niches;
Their boyfriends (by whom they were fondly referred to as *bitches*)

All froze their smirks, ponced, pierced, or blissed
As they were, naturally, and wondering what they'd kissed.

The birthrate continued to decline. Muslim
Women sensibly refused marriage. A slim

Plurality, then, by early mid-century, achieved
Percentiles not seen since mitochondrial Eve.

If current trends continue, we project
Thinning holograms. These data have been double-checked.

LIBRARY UPDATE

Some light dereliction-season reading, pans and picks
For all you People of the Book. Don't miss Hans Blix,

Mastering PowerPoint: Chart and Bullet, his
Long awaited sequel to *Negative Capabilities.*

Also, Rommel & Rumsfeld: *Tanks in Sand;* C. LeMay:
Planes Over People. Both available on eBay,

In hard cover. Folks who liked these also liked *Perilous
Siege, Dolorous Stroke,* by Richard Perle,

And Edward Teller's *This Is the Church, This Is the Steeple.*
On a more serious note, try *People*

Of the Fiduciary Shore,
Also, *Turn Your Car into a Viable Domicile,* in-store

Only, at locations not so much near, as approaching.
On a related note, *I Ching*

And knucklebone dice
Sales hold strong. Perhaps on the rise.

ECUMENICAL

JERUSALEM, 2000

That bullets not splash festively
Against the Lexan screen
Where the grand mufti grins and waves
And the pope preens

(He's wearing purple, as it happens;
Patriarchal text.
The Mufti's sporting black, of course—
An architect)—

Let's pray for help and hit the mat
Where heaven's ironed out
With a hopeful heart for time to come
Without a doubt,

Where Middle East meets first West
At the Middle Sea, whose part
Has been a little crooked since
The very start.

And let us pray for this parade
Of fathers of our churches
And for their several holy books
And demiurges.

And for ourselves—may we survive
The Ecumenical,
Recalling Hardy's verses, viz.,
"The Man He Killed."

Who couldn't use a nipperkin
(My word, that word is odd)
To help dissolve his differences
Involving God?

As He/She/They once bent above
The primal soup tureen
To sniff one alphabetically
Unselfish gene

That such may smear some coverslip
A thousand years from now
In a world without apocalypse
Or sacred cow,

Bless pope and mufti. That's our prayer.
And as this prayer depends
On safety glass, bless also their
Mercedes-Benz.

THE JUDEO-CHRISTIAN TRADITION

Of *course* they'd need an
Omnipotent god. Look whom
He'd have to pardon.

CRITICAL

"The system's going critical!"
"The needle's in the red!"
"The warning lights . . . it's a Christmas tree . . ."
I forget what else he said.

The President's voice was oil on water;
It smoothed the heavy chop.
Our water we threw on petroleum fires
And found they didn't stop.

Well, the oil wars flickered out at last,
Though the water wars did not.
The gaffers missed the trees sometimes,
And some children who'd been shot.

But the snowdrop blooms in the dog urine
And the well, they say, is capped
Like the debt, or the vials of our lives
Where we prove that kids adapt.

The lab's a little smoky, true.
Our fate depends on cunning.
If the eyes tear up, put goggles on.
The experiment is running.

NOTED

Things I know are making me sick
In ways they didn't, once. The sliver

Of glass nuzzles deeper. Zinc
And mercury accumulate in the liver.

The heart?—a heat sink.
In the groin, the little elevator lift.

Money bores me even as it scares me. Racing
Pulse! What else does that? Some love.

Often I wish to sing,
When all I can manage is a laugh.

ASPHYXIATION SAPPHICS

Whoa, there, who's there, hosing his rooftop, staring
skyward, dumbstruck attitude oddly still, a
blank-eyed, statuary, afflicted pose? So
what in the hell is

going on here, anyway? Halley's Comet's
months away. No tactical warhead's scheduled
in. . . . Is Mount St. Helens about to blow her
chimney pot? Where's the

fire? Look—executives, lawyers, mothers,
looping jets of water on asphalt shingles,
cedar shakes—whole neighborhoods, hosing hazy
radioactive

rainbows, oh, already the windshield's starred with
fallen night, sweet ladybug, pray now heaven's
hook-and-ladder company comes in time to
save us from drowning.

SEPTEMBER

All that gone up blood
somewhere in a white cloud bank
seeding next year's rain.

All that given blood
congealing in the glass tank.
All that lidocaine.

SEPARATED BY LITTLE BUT
AN ADEQUATE SENSE OF THE TRAGIC

We speak. My friend from Central Europe (Poland)
Where they've applied themselves to Blood Studies
In the University of Time,

And having dabbled in the horrible
And practiced on their kids, and whose custody
Has poisoned earth from the Oder to the Rhine,

Knows: *No Can Do.* The American faith is wrong:
Figment as it is of a Cinderella
Liberty, sired as it was by Seabees on sober

Prairie women, under sod, to the strong
Drone of the bone deacons. No surrender.
Sin is lassitude. Apply the spur

Of will to Yankee inwit, wink and thumbs-up,
Pal, no problem but proves tractable. . . .
But even love won't work, sometimes, he says,

The dirtiest surprise of all. Which about sums up
The unspeakable, which we never mentioned, tabled
Like the *International Trib* between us, all those days.

LESS LARKS

Ventricular plosives an ocean of jay
Adrift in the lit condition of May—

Dish of ginger?
Petal in a puddle?
A little wheatstraw
Stuck in the stocking?

I think I will and will not say—

An inch uninjured?
An orbit centripetal?
A tot of rye raw
In the talking?

I try to think the night won't nighten.
I try to dream the might from mightn't,
And think of our children, and pray.

PART EIGHT

FOLLY

SECURITY COUNCIL

[Simultaneous Translation]

The invisible paint on the warplanes peels like fly ash
On the moon. Soon the whites of their eyes. Attar
Of diesel drizzling the night. Light the antiaircraft
Battery: candelabrum of future knowledge. *[Oisin*

To Caelte, in the Black Book of Carrow Dhu.]

As for the butterfly on the fender of the tank:
Until further notice, let our conversations flutter
Hither and thither, disturbing weather patterns
Only on the far side of the amiable globe. *[T'ang*

Dynasty, c. 770, attributed to Tu Fu.]

A whole new style in war! Just cause! Low cost! Caw,
Caw! But in the sand that trickles out the hours,
All wars are old-style wars. Here's
A bayonet. Here's a belly. *[Archilochus*

To Korax, 645 B.C.; fragment titled "Fool."]

FALL OF ROME

In the ought-to-be-speechless hollow of the greatest church of its age,
Edging sideways under the skycool pitiless oculus of the deity
And in consideration of heaven and hell,
I overhear a woman whisper Harold, what's your HDL,
While an American kid with a toothpick and pecs
Kisses his strappy girl's tattoo, a (what else?)
Snake, while the Sony-eyed guy checks his pixels
And lumens and pans—
                          Pantheon, August 2000. Elsewhere,
Well, lots. The oracle closes at Delphi. I? I think of Mir
Scraping down the cobalt dome, also war hammers
At the altar font, the last aqueduct cut, recalling—
What?—reproductive vigor? Some miraculous
News—bad health—earthquake, maybe, weakened revetments, priests
Pointing mortar at Constantinople, Attila's horse veering east.

ALARIC INTELLIGENCE MEMO #36

Their women are whores; their men are boys,
Stalled to inertia by infinite choice.
They live in a hell of marvels: fierce,
Fully automated joys.

The prowess of their engineers
Is justly fabled. They've leapt to the nearest
Lamps of night. Such chasms spanned!—
Too black for all but their blindest seers.

Their warrior class, insufficiently manned,
Is mad, responsive, and under command.
Their weapon of choice is the toggle switch.
Be watchful. They kill with either hand.

They diddle themselves to a sexual scorch
From middle childhood through advanced age,
To worship the Mother, conceptualized
As a green severity bearing a torch.

Their gods are tripes, cradled inside,
Served by a priesthood garbed in white
Who sometimes remove them with sharpened spoons,
And cast them away. I cannot say why.

Their poetry barks. Their faith, a ruins,
Ghost-infested, affords no womb
Of future. In sum: however skilled,
They are overripe. My Lord, strike soon.

Addendum: proud to have served your will,
I have lived too long among them. I am ill.
I am infected with dreams. At the first moon
Of conquest, I respectfully request to be killed.

Herewith committed to blood rune
By Agent 36, without witness or wergild
This first Sunday of the Tooth Month,
Praise God, of God's Year One.

IF BEV ABOVE

The sizzle of the gas grill calls *Mitch, hon,*
And he, teary (as we may imagine)
In the kitchen chopping onions

Answers *Hmmm?* may not their household gods
Grin to see that shrink-wrapped, half-thawed ingot
Of blood succeeding so from fridge to sink

To smoke, the kids to fireflies and croquet?
And lip-synch these good-hearted heartland folk
Like karaoke? Such accord! Could *OK*

Be their word for half a world away
What here might seem more inconsiderate—
To fill a perfect stranger's Saturday,

Without respect to one's immortal soul,
With a carbureted bloom or aerosol
Of metal slivers and sheet fire, in error?

MEANWHILE,

Convinced the shish kebabs were code, Kyle
Spent the balance of the barbecue
Considering their permutations. Mushroom—
Onion—cherry tomato—mushroom . . . *(hmmm)* . . . lamb-cube—
Lamb-cube . . . *(lamb-cube?!)* Meanwhile, Barb and Sherm
Perplexed the data stream with subtle guile,

Interpolating peppers in a sequence
Which might have been random, or apparently random, one simply
Couldn't be certain. Hence Vince's increasing unease
Respecting security, re: the water supply
(And it's such *good* water, too), and Dick and Sunny's
Darkening smiles. Who knows. The beef . . . the oil. . . . Ill winds

Do blow. Consensus spread throughout the yard:
American forces must strike soon, and strike hard.

IN A PIG'S EYE

Former Deputy Defense Secretary Paul Wolfowitz,
Dressed casually in alligator clips and a hood,
Took questions again today from the Senate Subcommittee
For the Belated Investigation of What's
Going On. Mr. Wolfowitz repeated that he had first heard
Senior Foreign Policy Architect Walter Mitty
Present the philosophical underpinnings for war in October
2001, making swooping motions with his hand, and helicopter-
Noises with his mouth. "I believe he also said *Bup-*
Bup-bup-bup-bup-bup," added Mr. Wolfowitz. Dober-
man pinschers continued the questioning, while his captors
Discussed among themselves the uncharacteristically abrupt
Tone Mr. Cheney had taken, assessing his own
Performance. "Great God," he'd said Tuesday, "what have I done?"

WHAT WENT WRONG IN IRAQ?

But sexy
is Rick Steves!
sighs the war–
weary ex–
Rumsfeld slut, surfing
the briefings.

O muse, TV's
a murmur of shame
but a shimmer
indeed.

And foreign
adventure was ever a question
of leaving
and grieving.

And alarums
and clarions
for risen is Alaric
and the heart of the human
is a licked
reed.

A POT OF TEA

Loose leaves in a metal ball
Or men in a shark cage steeping,
Ideas stain the limpid mind
Even while it's sleeping:

Ginseng or the scent of lymph
Or consequences queasing
Into wide awareness, whence,
Like an engine seizing

Society remits a shudder
Showing it has feeling,
And the divers all have shaving cuts
And the future's in Darjeeling—

Blind, the brain stem bumps the bars
Of the shark cage, meanwhile, feeding,
And the tea ball's cracked, its leaves cast
To catastrophic reading:

Ideas are too dangerous.
My love adjusts an earring.
I take her in my arms again
And think of Hermann Göring,

And all liquidities in which
A stain attracts an eating,
And of my country's changing heart,
And hell, where the blood is sleeting.

JUDGMENT

Ungravity!—the war graves flying open again—
Imagine (spin the watchstem): a sort of reverse sneeze,
Whole clouds of the little nursling, breast-nestled
Bullets drifting free again like wind-borne spores
Whose sudden disappearance up the gun,
As though that were a kind of vacuum nozzle,
Amazes all capable of performing this porn-
ographic miracle of recall, this absorbed sob—
Such the automatic recoil in us all.
But better stop. The figure's riveting. Now a Nazi
Walking backwards into his mother. The Serb
Zips. Hell fire refills the reserve nacelle—
Jet fuel's liquefaction. To lips, words.
Uncatapulted pilot, shock-haired, grinning, backwards.

OPEN LETTER

Washington, Madison, Jefferson,
And that amateur lot
Had the quixotic notion

That if ever our sons
Were to be shipped off to get shot
In the service of the nation

It really shouldn't ought
To be by a senior, insulated clique
Of high-level office temps

And their short-term CEO. That's what
The Constitution says, silly thing. Meanwhile, clock
Ticks. Fool fumbles matches in the gasoline dumps.

King's horses quiver and flare; elsewhere, thought
Flags. Flags snap. Blood sumps in the legs, and clogs.
Dumb

The great nation in its camouflage pajamas and clerk's
Soul accepts that cold thermometer,
The market survey, inserted to the hilt.

Are we melancholic or choleric
Today? Shall the doctors work the mass murder
Side of the street, the Hitler

Thing? Or rather *Law & Order,* a mid-
Term issue? Will it be Good v. Evil,
Today, as in *The Two Towers? Shane?*

Is this a sequel, for mature
Audiences? The pupil of the Oval
Office dilates to full size, changed

Utterly. Tether the children. Caesar's master-
Minds whisper and confer: they work their awful
Divinations, searching for a product name.

Up! Up on your hind legs, timorous Congress! To waffle
Harrumphing and slink amongst an enervated
Pack of palace

Eunuchs dishonors your oath, if nothing else: war falls
To *you;* check the parchment. Heart's never
In long supply, but please, a pulse

In the wrist, inner
Something-or-other! Because later, when the sword
Of righteous retribution's collateral slaughter

Of innocents executed in our
Name trebles September's toll, when the sorties
Shrieking off the carriers clatter

Our glassware at breakfast, lunch, and dinner
And drinks and snacks and dessert
Amidst the canned laughter

And commercials and occasional dizzying
Grief of another kid dead for why again?—surely
Something-fine-or-else-he-was-a-chump—

That exhausting hero-machine—while dust
To dust, the American blitzkrieg as usual
Continues to fail to finish the job

—*recapitation,* was it?—as who shall
Hold that archaic smile when Iraq shatters
Like a piñata full of bees

And conflagration spreads, and the jewel
Of liberty darkens, and the world howls murder
And glancing that way for once we can't place

Any of their faces, and maybe eventually
Jowls atremble the president is heard to mutter
This isn't what I meant, at all—
                                        Well, bless

Us, that will be too late. The scimitar's
Unscabbarded: martyr
Yourselves if necessary, Senators. It's roll call.

SEATTLE TIMES, OCTOBER 2002

MORE POLITICS

They sealed the pact with a worm inside,
And knew what they were doing.
It wasn't that they were wicked; in fact,
They said it was that, or nothing.

And we haven't died, and we're still intact,
Though still we feel it stirring;
Though they stitched the wound with a worm inside
It may yet come to nothing.

PART NINE

EPHEMERIS

HERMETIC SAPPHICS

Sir! Old Wingfoot, Quicksilver, salve the day gone
Pink—O Road-God! Mercury pools, the highway's
Slick mirage. . . . Well, traveler's stomach, call it.
Succor the carsick

Soul, its breastplate's Volkswagen alp escutcheon
Shrinking so: no optic illusion: one thing
Less and sunshine quitting the face of one we
Maybe admired or

Were or . . . Janus-faced is the maladjusted
Sky a rear-view mirror receding. . . . Say which
Object may be closer than it appears? The
Vanishing point, sir.

ABETTORS OF ENTROPY

All of them: not just the *dys*, the *un*, the ineffectually shot-
Home bolt, sugared petroleum, wrench in the works, wars, but abettors
Of entropy in all their shades and cools and shorts:

All floor hair balls, furbelows of dream, butter-
Smear on the refrigerator grate, dog-nose
On the windshield like the weatherman's turbid

Satellite map, mayonnaise
Spoon in the sink, that sprung hinge
Banged a touch too good and hard, mayhem

In the sock drawer, door ajar, derangements,
All the little proofs that the general case
Has suffered somewhat for our recent passage. Strange,

Should a gum wrapper's glim foil blink on the golf course
Cause one so to feel the reciprocating engines
Of fate. Again, inertia, shin-deep in the quartz

Movement of it. Entropy. Chance
Action from the appalled boudoir to the swabbed
Apothecary beaker of heaven, that plasma churn,

That sad gas-sluice, abattoir
Of stars. Where now a sudden wink:
A retinal nick, a jot of a jet, a war-

Plane boiled out of African bauxite, by Boeing,
Maybe, balled up and rolled between those quern-
Stones, sky and plate, heat death and Big Bang,

If that's the story, still. Hard to believe. An urn;
A few effects; a desk, its gravity collapsed
In a couple of cardboard cartons in the barn,

And that's the Father. And they say nothing in the blue apse
Of time like him. And the Mother a scrap of a lullaby,
Maybe, a silver hairpin, and nothing, no ionized urp

Of matter, plasma jet, jot nor dollop nor lobbed
Tittle of starshine cobwebbed in a coalsack,
No difference but smoothed, no endless digits of pi

But won't end up like them, the Mother, the Father, exactly.

OFFICE VISIT

On the day he died, not ninety, quite,
partially blind, in chronic pain and jacket
and tie my dad said no energy. He just
had none. *A courteous old guy,*

thought the doctor. *The contained kind. Quiet.*
Then the doctor, perhaps educated
elsewhere, checking his watch, suggested
Exercise. You might try yoga.

NEVERMORE

Look at the struck magnet's
lost force

look at the bleach-splashed map
whose deserts advance

as Caliban's comet-streaked
prehistoric island

gathers like an asterisk
of iron filings

floating antimatter
in the eye of Vermeer's

mind-bound geometer
as *nevermore*

was the raven's ridiculous croak
it's a stroke, O Father

pitching backwards to the floor.

ALBA RED

Hung vial IV morphine drip

hummingbird feeder
where the cats can't get it

long brake light occluded in billowing exhaust
in the chill predawn fog of a final
wish in the world,

and the sun rising through it.

EPHEMERIS

The compass steeple
shivers in its shrine; nine
lights rise the sky's skull
still, curl again across our palled sleep's
pillowslip, this little night drawn close around the known
world, where you're not, now—
nor scale

to show birds heavier
in flight, nor kissed teacup
cast adrift in the awful vale
of the First Law, veering
left or right in its new insentience—

chance again, then: no
omen, no more known world's whatnot,
all those silly, lovely bibelots
loose in their sockets
now, so much unknit wit
now, and this ink circuit
blown:

blue dome, smoke—
lit, wisps of a new incense—
hands—a skidding teacup—
trick mirror's oval veil—

how could we, ankle deep in the filling shovel
of the here below,
believe?—or we, with our mirror optics
and pitiful, wishful field equations so encrypt

tongue and lip, little undulant air-anemone
of the last vowel—
gone—no Cupid's tongued *O, Q,*
calling out to *U* forever, ring,
pierced ring—
where there is no attraction anymore
among such things.

FOR JAMES MERRILL

HONOR GUARD

To speak love in the teeth of death was natural.
Here, hair nor raiment rent, nothing wrung nor gnashed.
Families assembled in the simple wish to be sure all

Emotional needs were met in the forms of the funeral.
The needs of the many need not nod to the needs of the few,
Narrowly construed, nor were all

Musics to be cut from the rain of the ancient keening.
Who knew the casketed colonel in dress blues, shaven and seen,
Or the baby, who flew from afar for this, unready for weaning,

Or the daughters who remembered the life of the one a weapon
Who'd thundered their yonder, whose time had never been once upon?
Penitent not for themselves, then, they wept and they wept,

Which, unplanned as it was, blent well with the haunt
Of taps through the settling rifle smoke, and the ancient sound
The baby cut from the sky, in pressure descending.

METAMORPHOSIS

Weary dinner; drone
of voices fuzzes . . .

by candlelight lift
translucent tracery

of fishbone free
of the white fillet, a weir

of bone, cobweb of bone. . . .
Bring dream: by night

the ancient unchanging
imago again

where at long last, wire-sharp
and Mylar–light

the wingblades sigh sine-
clean through muscle and gristle,

quick and skin,
strike air, refract in it,

snap taut, and lift . . . lifting
behind spine

and thready filamentous
nerve net out,

the whole blue, blind,
iridescent dragonfly of it

sucked up
into blues and high violets

we fail to follow
with our eyes, but only

as a fading electrical trace
in the mucid slap

of the landed heart
beating back the ground.

CUMAEAN

Without realizing he had arrived
at such a juncture in his life,

healthy, if half-blind,

he found himself at Cumae, where had been
a Sibyl. *Is this all, then,*

he was inclined

to ask. No more answer
than expected. A lazy gabble of silence,

and that was in his mind.

FOUR SCORE

My first time at Tarot I was a Page,
Of course; at cards one ought to look one's age.

A score of years flipped by. One smoky night
I quested through the future as a Knight.

What face to put on twenty more? My ring
And grizzle-gravitas marked me a King.

My question: Cups; Coins; Wands; Swords.
My answer: the rattlesnake of shuffling cards.

KNIGHT, DEATH, DEVIL

Young in front of Dürer
I knew *Knight*, naturally.
That's me, in a while. Why, though, *Devil*

When the greater horror, *Death*, old shudder-
Bones, bags us anyway? Surely
A redundancy, this double-

Jeopardy? So a soldier
Thinks, who hasn't yet felt the chilly
Mandible.

Consider "integrity"—! That durable
Absurdity, erect, individual,
Primitive, the true man's

Trait, innate and terrible,
The pure verge
Of character, like a lion mane

Or eagle eye or light step to the stirrup,
Oh, the chest a forge
And a man one thing without remainder.

[Note: Dürer, Reader, sees the
Knight no youth,
Ever as I thought, eye on the scythe.]

PART TEN

RINGS

ALBA BAD

The moon is a mess in the baobab tree
A smear along the limb
A cracked rib, loose, white
Licked thin.

Overhead a few stars
Crawl across the calm:
Sweat bees licking blacking
Off God's palm.

Sun an aneurism now
Above the crater's rim
Where dawn spreads like a slick
From a leaking drum.

What good can ever come of this,
Love, let's light;
Without the words it's only gas
Against the night.

THAT WAS GRIM KING

And where have thee been then, John, these ten years past?
Ah, the journeyman's smile: Life, with its customary pistol-

up-the-nose approach, having determined
you were, while (mind

you) not altogether without talent,
much requiring deepening, commenced to dredge. Tollund

Man on a stirrup-couch, reclining. Like what? Not
tongue depressors, *aahhh*, not oto-

pharyngeal flashlight, quite, nor bollock-
cough, corneal air-puff gun, *pop*, not the old umbilicus-

tug-and-cut, quite, nor waking up to waxed linoleum *clack
clack*, exactly, those approaching footsteps, the old *oh, look,*

*Life again, in scrubs and steel spectacles, and none too gentle,
are we ticklish today?* No. Nor macular poke, nor digital

manipulation, not cheek peeled back in the sunless
glare of the klieg light, not bed-crank ratchet, tic-tic, listen—

the sough of the little laugh in the linen mask—
not that, nor what, mosquito-

whine of high-speed dentistry, etc.,
nor smoke melanoma hissing under its soldering

150

iron, that laser-lick, nor worse, the slick
lip-smack of the latex glove, that lubricant, businesslike

prostatic jab, John, imagining a raffish
wink behind—no, none of those mortifying, awful orificial

probes, precisely, those hard exhales.
Howl,

John,
you gentle-

man, not so much for the lying waiting this raw touch
or that violation, this as-it-turned-out unnecessary curettage

of the mitral valves, that membrane-flick of the inside-
out eyelid, not as you can see anything so sudden

as a flung drape, floodlit, cupped hand braceleted
and pinned back, exposing everything, though not love not least,

last.

RINGS

I

ENVOY:
UNEASY

The poem is no fun.
It wears heavy plate—
plutonium—
so out of place
here in the mango glade.
An awkwardness for us,
truth to tell.
Until hell:
until the blade
slits the forest
and underneath earth
melts.

Now the dense
dwarf poem scythes forth,
shears time at the hilt,
fends fire, folds
us in its fool
moon-suit embrace
and drops the smoky mica visor clang.

Maybe suckling
we wake safe
a decade later
in another frangipani place,
eyeing the uneasy poem.

II

NEVER
Say never, never, never,
and already the effort

of will against world
works open a seam old

as lies, familiar
as falling.

FINGER
EXERCISE
Why would this blood-badged
man (a hero, he in whom
honed
aptitudes of will, habituated

over a lifetime, so outstrip
the habit of life
itself) lift
his bib cravat, rip

his buttons, punch
those blunt
fingers through the paper lantern
of the chest and pinch

the leaping artery's warm wick
so? So snuff life,
leaving
him white as wax

and fit for no ring's signet?
Instinct.

III

True: at certain temperatures and pressures
surface physics ceases to apply.

AT CERTAIN
TEMPERATURES
AND PRESSURES Apples fall up. The Good Yeoman
yowls like cut veal. The Good Wife

writhes all the salt dark long
wrong, and the wrung moon rises, and the green star sets.

Certain of little in these times, we
sweep eyeless mice out of their nests.

Noose traps. Listen all night where the doe rat,
rotating queerly in the granary, paddles and pants,

and the killed buck rat giggles and clacks in his sleep.

The primate, chemically decorticate,
commenced to nuzzle and droom. The familiar cat

OLD STORY,
END OF rose off his lap like powder smoke, *puff*
in a breeze, and gone. Catlike, too, his perfect

friend licked her fingers and left. The room
was silent then, except for the hushing of a far-off broom.

IV

Blue flash passion
god-sent

SHAME

shaman with his calabash
prescient

man in the basement
face intent

shakes heaven gently—
tchssh, tchssh—

to check the filament.

A god's blue fire gone, the man is left like a page
in the grate, apparently unchanged. Ash-

ASH

gray, granted, and somewhat curled at the edge,
but readable. Readable, he thinks. Until the passage—

cat's paw?—backwash?—up the chimney?—*whump-
whump*, rotorblades of a distant hummingbird,
let's say: then all at once, old cobweb upwhipped,
the words vanish. Now this man is without words.

V

RECURRING
NIGHTMARE

Another sweaty pillowslip wadding
another cold moon's musketball
down the long barrel
of the open pupil. Wet flint. Coward.

NOTHING GOOD
OR BAD BUT
SAYING MAKES
IT SO

Here's a prised-open letter
with a little
night-chink sky inside, spit-

shut. Luck:
the log–
drag on the splintered tibia. Long–

bones heal.
Inhale
deeply. This is nowhere near Hell.

156

VI

ANOTHER
DRINKING
SONG

Here's a flagon for whose affliction
licks the deep far-back,
the membrane of the angel
the crumpled venom sac.

Where the lipless smile of addiction
whispers *we're all the same,*
and the tongue of the monitor lizard
flickers like a flame.

CLOSE
YOUR
EYES

See lizard tongue like an altar candle. Clutch
your mother's sleeve. Close your eyes and wish.

Watch wrinkled vulture neck now.
See Satyr and Centaur slobber and pinch.

Watch leather wing shaking out now,
vascularizing purply and moist. Inch

away. Watch devil growing like tissue culture,
skin in a dish.

VII

Brown recluse spider by
the unfound Easter egg.

NINE

THINGS

Argyle sock
on the Mohave highway.

Wee toad poison
seeping through a Kleenex.

Claimed person
kissing the next.

Debriding memory, love,
so much pale, numb

LONG

EMBALM

flesh sloughs.

Laugh up his mouth who vilifies.

Squeeze out the white maggots, lies.
Burst them with the thumb-
nail. Lick the palm. Shut the eyes.

VIII

Stick a screwdriver into my face twice.
Those are my eyes.

TRUTH

Club with the muffled hammer—there,
and there: those my ears.

Break my mouth against the curb.
Now I have words.

I would gods solve for grace and mercy.
I see screwdrivers. Hammers

my dreams. The world there is no Lethe
for this. I speak teeth.

Now we are in the nucleus
of lead.

WHERE WE
ARE NOW

The cold floor glistens.

But no drip, drip. No phosphor-lit
wick. No distant doorclang. Listen:
no little scritchy rat-claws

on flagstone. No bat-flit. No bars.
No little window.

IX

CODA

I tried lacing loss into these lines,
thinking to bind it safely there.

But when much lifetime had raced by, I
saw rather

trapped in the scrag noose, too,
joy and daylight.

I bottled also bile in these poems,
thinking to isolate

the toxin. But when much lifetime had raced by, I
found it on the mantel.

I thought to lower these poems into a salt dome—
stable, it's said, for aeons.

And who isn't one?
Once

I tried to write invisibly,
but all lifetime is a candle.

PART ELEVEN

COMPASS ROSE

DARK MATTER

There is dark matter because how can there not be?
As phlogiston and ether, so dark matter. I believe
In all of them. That also, when we leave, we leave,

Because how can we not? As phlogiston
To the almond eye of the match, what aqueous logic
In the little flame-shaped tear? What physics chastens

That liquidity with its little wetness? What's
A never-was-nor-ever-could-be?—Quetzalcoatl;
Phoenix. What's was-but-gone-nor-evermore?—those squadrons

Of pterosaurs. What's is-but-hardly-ever?—river-
Fishing owl by daylight. If a wing-width is the severance
Between such things, that only—then which are these: the lover's

Long gaze, the lover's very long love, or
Perfect love, another ether, or dark matter on a salver?

ALBA BEACH

Hardy thing this waiting, love.
Bivalve glisten of the last of the cloud-nestling moon . . .
think of the knife's unnatural plunge toward the palm
to open such a cold thing!
Pin-lit ferry
caught in the tidal set
against the shadow shore beyond,
constellated, slow, zodiacal
as sky scrolls up its interminable purples,
pulling west.
Mitral click of the shell-shore's outreach,
nearing ebb.
Bill of the heron.
Eyelash-lick of the sweep hand.
Eventual sun
to the floodplain in the chest.

PARALLEL WORLD

And if the world had gone marsupial?
What then? Ask Madagascar. A "rat,"
A "wolf," a "lion," even. The simple soup

Of possibility, whose iterations
Vary or converge . . . I read owlish shamans'
Theories of the multiverse, wherein errata

Fork forth worlds, each ort of dumb chance
Exfoliating clones, they say, like craze-
Lines in a shocked pane. . . . Such origins

As who can't say just so, if the sums agree?
Mathematical physicists! Mad
As hatters, those guys. As for vagary—

Love, who believes in "love," which "is," or "are"—?
I don't want to live in Madagascar.

ASYMMETRIES

Dreaming such asymmetries
So unlike dreams themselves, or thoughts
Reversible as billiard shots,
Or so they've seemed—

Asymmetries in time: the cream
Unmixing from the stirred tea;
The words unspeaking in the martyr's
Mouth; the first crime

Unconceived. A cemetery's
Serried teeth, and live nerve
At each root. Small mutterings
Which swarm the stone of the Senate's

High, white, marble dome, down
The curve and, falling mute, remind
Us of asymmetries: the skulls
Beneath the Great Tree,

Their mound uncorbeling in air,
The carpels closing on the fruit,
The tree's unbearing, pulse, pulse,
And green slip and shoot.

ENTROPY OVER

Is memory entropy imperfectly backwards? Why, who've
We here? See, Childhood simpers up; the toxic windsock
Of a nebulosity's sucked back some cosmic Hoover-

Hose, and who's that again? Your parents? That in the whole blue apse
Of time never was a wonder like them, nor nothing, no zigzag
Waveblip nor—what was it?—quantum urps, chance oops,

Nor anything of any sort that won't end up exactly
Like them, and you also, by the end of this story, pitch-
Forked chaffish into some windy postgalactic coalsack?—

Each undirected or sidelong perfectly or perpetually
Shot-home reproach, the gas-whisper, the log-drag of the ugly
Word, the wrench-in-the-works, sugared petroleum, botched

Smile, malefaction, the major heat death of marriage—
All of it—the whole cold hologhast
Gone to quietude, though not yet, luckily, luckily.

MID

Long drive between two oceans, love.
As the muddy Mississippi
to the Mid-Cretaceous Seaway, so
this reduced day,
this little arterial leap
to the crazy gone time
of the rough of love
where neither concentration nor
sleep. Since
then, it's true, there
has been sleep between us.
Speech, too—much
if not always too much or enough.
So I say harrumph, for emphasis. Is it so far
between those putative northernmost worst
hurricanes of Earthly history—
cyclonic storms in these high latitudes! Lord,
what neaps and floods and unfamiliar
creatures tickled the womb of the lukewarm
prairie then—and that
salt flat
we're said to be desiccating toward?
What to make of that threat
but this kiss
and another hundred miles before we too-weary
retumble, and damn the tomb?

HYDROLOGY; LACHRYMATION

The river meanders because it can't think.
Always, with the river, the path of least resistance.
Look: lip of a low bowl swerves the river tens
Or thousands of miles wild. The least brink
Of a ridge and its python shies. . . . How efficient—think—
Would a straight sluice to the sea be, in terms
Computable? When's water simpler? Cisterns
Certainly, still as a tearful blink;
Lake effects likewise, like the great circular storms,
Tornadoes, hurricanes; those lesser weather systems
Too, troubling the benthos where the ice caps shrink.
Straightforward isotherms . . . or is it isotheres . . .
But a moment ago, someone mentioned tears.
Why tears, for love? Why rivers? I can't think.

THE WINTER

Not dawn on Christmas Day. Who writes the rest?

The stars withdraw their needles from the night.
The moon, a melted compress, cools the west.
The dark unbandages the earth. Inert,

Awake, we touch a face. What is the truest
Thing, Time or Love? We know the body
Won't be healed whole. The altruist

Won't waken from his nightmare into beauty.
But what else is a proper song to sing?
Somewhere witches writhe the Sabbat, hooting.

Somewhere pornographers are practicing
Their thrilling synecdoches, all hands going
Down again in glory. Far off, tossing

In his sheets, a seer tries unknowing.

And still! And still!—there lives the dearest freshness

Steep down the amygdala,
And though some poets won't but more ferocious
Black deracinations of a dully

Dollar-wild world abide, ambrosias
Yet decant. They do. I had a little daughter
Last October. I bought three dozen roses.

I'm not the only one. The auditors
Of others' suffering don't care, of course—
Who has time for everything? The cauter

Of the sunrise pinks or scars all augurs'
Eyes the same. Hole in the retina!—who'd
Wish it? I see things, too. If that's a curse,

It's cast in light of large unsimple gratitudes.

FOR RICHARD WILBUR

CONTRACTION

One thousand one . . . one thousand two—I wonder

Too, at the queer displacement of effect:
The butterfly, its far typhoon, the kiss,
Its tears. What parachutes down from a fact.
I wonder how my luck has come to this.

Contractual arrangements built on laws
Of nature, sure, if nature's what we are,
Or have, somehow. Womb seizes. Why? Because
A wooze of hydrogen annealed its star,

Once, here comes rain, maybe. Now seven weeks
Too soon our baby at the bone gate shies.
That's *right now*. Breathe. What daughter wakes
Into tomorrow's dream? What's that, love? She's—

One thousand three . . . one thousand four . . . far thunder.

LATE CHILD

Lost art:
hope's hoops
recoopering
those gone days'
stove staves,
O
again
oaken as
an acorn
heart!

PATHETIC FALLACY

The rocks look wrinkled
and the sea, sore

and what do the willows
know of war?

The king in his orchid
curdles noon

till the stars are salt
in the western wound.

And when and when
the baby cries

the moon leaks milk
in the rooster skies,

and so and so
till morn is eve

once more as ever
but make believe.

ACKNOWLEDGMENTS, CHIMERAS, NOTES

I want to thank editors and publishers who presented many of these poems in their first form. These include *The Antioch Review* ("New Year, with Nipperkin"), *The Cincinnati Review* ("Grasshopper," "Sky with Eagles," "Asymmetries"), *Cranky* ("Ecumenical Song"), *Cream City Review* ("Asphyxiation Sapphics"), *The Great River Review* ("Mid," "The Rough"), *Long Journey: Contemporary Northwest Poets* ("Pathetic Fallacy"), *The New Criterion* ("New"), *The New England Review* ("Biographical," "Abettors of Entropy"), *The New Yorker* ("Coda," "Alba Red"), *Poetry* ("0,1," "Now We Are Ready to Speak of Bodies Changing into Other Bodies"), *Poetry Northwest* ("Rear View," "Surrealism," "Muse Interviews," "Shall I Compare Thee to Appearances," "Turbulence," "Entropy Over," "Resonance"), *The Seattle Times* ("Open Letter"), *The Sewanee Review* ("Honor Guard"), *Subtropics* ("Lives of the Romantics" "Lightning Strikes the Protein-Rich Precambrian Tide Pool," "Volkerwanderung Again"), *TriQuarterly* ("Fall of Rome," "Alaric Intelligence Memo #36"), *Verse* ("More Longitude," "Per Benjamin Franklin"), and *The Yale Review* ("Ephemeris," "Rewrite," "Scenes").

I am particularly grateful for oases of calm time generously and crucially afforded by the Liguria Study Center for the Arts in Bogliasco and the Helen Riaboff Whiteley Center in Friday Harbor.

For any measure in which this book's tonal experiments resolve as a poetic whole, I wish to credit Cody Walker. I'd have been worse confused without his subtle readings, brilliant insights, and generous counsel.

Additional notes and optional color commentary—not to impugn the poems' self-sufficiency in the eyes of those who require it, but just for those who appreciate a word or two behind the hand:

Gray Goose and Gander from Mother Goose. What river has just one earthly shore? Encircling ocean is the traditional answer.

"Turbulence": The Heisenberg anecdote is often retold, though I learn it resembles another, involving the British physicist Horace Lamb, a little too closely to seem trustworthy. Lamb, in a talk before the British Association for the Advancement of Science, reportedly said, "I am an old man now, and when I die and go to heaven there are two matters on which I hope for enlightenment. One is quantum electrodynamics, and the other is the turbulent motion of fluids. And about the former I am rather optimistic." Mars rocks were found in the Antarctic: more turbulence.

"The Rough": The actual lines from *As You Like It* 5.2.38–40 (partly emended in "Mid") read "They are in the very wrath of love, and will together. Clubs cannot part them."

"Balancing": It was Bishop Berkeley who spoke of the tree falling in the forest, in consideration of the silence, not the dizziness.

"More Charles": In biological terms, a chimera is distinguished from a hybrid. Hybrids can be made the old-fashioned way: their phenotype typically presents a sort of smooth average of the differing parents' traits. Always artificial, by contrast, a chimera is a discontinuous mixture—woolly here, scaly there. This book is a chimera.

"Scenes": Unlike metals, in brine, make a battery. The "nobler" metal accepts ions, the "baser" metal gives them up, corroding. Here, copper punctures aluminum.

"Ecumenical": In 2000, Pope John Paul II did have a historic meeting with the grand mufti of Jerusalem, but the motorcade is a fantasy.

"Security Council": "The Black Book"—the Tu Fu—the Archilochus fragment—all imaginary.

"Fall of Rome": The earthquake attracting Attila to Constantinople was historical. The Oracle closed in 392.

"What Went Wrong in Iraq?" recalls a short-lived media titillation respecting former secretary of defense Donald Rumsfeld, summed up in this citation: "CNN called him a 'virtual rock star.' Fox dubbed him a beltway 'babe magnet.' And *The Wall Street Journal* hailed 'the new hunk of home-front airtime,' says Jennifer Harper, media columnist for *The Washington Times*. 'He's got that steady gaze, that strong jaw—a man you could trust if all hell were breaking loose. That's pretty sexy stuff.' " [*People Weekly*, December 2, 2002]

"A Pot of Tea": Here again is Hermann Göring's famous quote: "Naturally, the common people don't want war . . . but after all it is the leaders of a country who determine the policy, and it is always a simple matter to drag the people along, whether it is a democracy, or a fascist dictatorship, or a parliament, or a communist dictatorship. Voice or no voice, the people can always be brought to the bidding of the leaders. That is easy. All you have to do is to tell them they are being attacked, and denounce the pacifists for lack of patriotism and exposing the country to danger. It works the same in every country."

"Dark Matter" earns the quotes around it: as I understand things, astronomers can't find 96 percent of the universe, whose gravitation is necessary to balance the books in current cosmological theory. Hence undetectable "dark matter" and "dark energy" are posited.

"Parallel World": See "many-worlds interpretation," and "multiverse," about which some serious people, at least, are serious, though it sounds like poetry to me.

"Asymmetries": Quantum physics speaks of it (in a technical way) not only in the case of handedness ("parity") and electrical charge, but also with respect to time. Some events (like billiard ricochets) look the same if the film is reversed; others, as we know and rue, don't.

A NOTE ABOUT THE AUTHOR

Richard Kenney is the author of three previous books of poetry: *The Evolution of the Flightless Bird*, *Orrery*, and *The Invention of the Zero*. He teaches at the University of Washington and lives with his family in Port Townsend.

A NOTE ON THE TYPE

The text of this book was set in Ehrhardt, a typeface based on the specimens of "Dutch" types found at the Ehrhardt foundry in Leipzig. The original design of the face was the work of Nicholas Kis, a Hungarian punch cutter known to have worked in Amsterdam from 1680 to 1689. The modern version of Ehrhardt was cut by the Monotype Corporation of London in 1937.

Composed by Creative Graphics, Allentown, Pennsylvania

Printed and bound by Thomson-Shore, Dexter, Michigan

Designed by M. Kristen Bearse